TABLES
FACTS & FIGURES

by Jacqueline Dineen
illustrated by John Dillow

CONTENTS

INTRODUCTION

This book is designed to help children to learn their times tables quickly and effectively by showing them the number patterns in each table.

The book is also a useful reference work about numbers in general. It tells how numbers and alphabets first came about, how and why people began to measure things, and how measurement developed from early times to the present day. Children will discover how ancient people measured time and divided the year up into months and seasons, how the first calendars came into existence, and what the first clocks were like. There is useful information about weight, length, capacity and area – and each section contains a few fascinating (and sometimes surprising!) facts relating to numbers.

At the back of the book is a section of helpful information, including washing machine and oven temperatures, clothing sizes and world currencies.

ALL THE TWOS

1	2	3	4	5	6	7	8	9	10
11	12	13	14	15	16	17	18	19	20
21	22	23	24	25	26	27	28	29	30
31	32	33	34	35	36	37	38	39	40
41	42	43	44	45	46	47	48	49	50
51	52	53	54	55	56	57	58	59	60
61	62	63	64	65	66	67	68	69	70
71	72	73	74	75	76	77	78	79	80
81	82	83	84	85	86	87	88	89	90
91	92	93	94	95	96	97	98	99	100

The numbers in pink show the pattern of the 2 times table. What do you notice about the numbers in the pink columns?

2 two   2nd second

Word	Meaning
double	two times as much
pair	two matching items
bicycle	two-wheeled cycle
tandem	cycle for two people
duet	song or music for two voices or instruments
twins	two children born at the same birth
couplet	two lines of verse
twice	two times

8

2 times table

$$0 \times 2 = 0$$
$$1 \times 2 = 2$$
$$2 \times 2 = 4$$
$$3 \times 2 = 6$$
$$4 \times 2 = 8$$
$$5 \times 2 = 10$$
$$6 \times 2 = 12$$
$$7 \times 2 = 14$$
$$8 \times 2 = 16$$
$$9 \times 2 = 18$$
$$10 \times 2 = 20$$
$$11 \times 2 = 22$$
$$12 \times 2 = 24$$

ALL THE THREES

1	2	3	4	5	6	7	8	9	10
11	12	13	14	15	16	17	18	19	20
21	22	23	24	25	26	27	28	29	30
31	32	33	34	35	36	37	38	39	40
41	42	43	44	45	46	47	48	49	50
51	52	53	54	55	56	57	58	59	60
61	62	63	64	65	66	67	68	69	70
71	72	73	74	75	76	77	78	79	80
81	82	83	84	85	86	87	88	89	90
91	92	93	94	95	96	97	98	99	100

The numbers in orange show the pattern of the 3 times table. What do you notice about the orange numbers going downwards? Are they even or odd? What is the difference between each number and the one below it?

Tri- comes from the Latin and Greek words for 'three'.

3 three   3rd third

Word	Meaning
treble, triple	three times as much; threefold
trio	three people singing or playing instruments
triplets	three children born at the same birth
tripod	a stand, stool or table on three feet or legs
tricycle	a three-wheeled cycle
trilogy	a three-part play or book
triangle	a three-sided flat shape
thrice	three times

3 times table

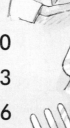

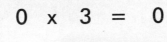
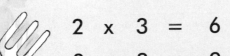

$$0 \times 3 = 0$$
$$1 \times 3 = 3$$
$$2 \times 3 = 6$$
$$3 \times 3 = 9$$
$$4 \times 3 = 12$$
$$5 \times 3 = 15$$
$$6 \times 3 = 18$$
$$7 \times 3 = 21$$
$$8 \times 3 = 24$$
$$9 \times 3 = 27$$
$$10 \times 3 = 30$$
$$11 \times 3 = 33$$
$$12 \times 3 = 36$$

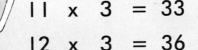

ALL THE FOURS

1	2	3	4	5	6	7	8	9	10
11	12	13	14	15	16	17	18	19	20
21	22	23	24	25	26	27	28	29	30
31	32	33	34	35	36	37	38	39	40
41	42	43	44	45	46	47	48	49	50
51	52	53	54	55	56	57	58	59	60
61	62	63	64	65	66	67	68	69	70
71	72	73	74	75	76	77	78	79	80
81	82	83	84	85	86	87	88	89	90
91	92	93	94	95	96	97	98	99	100

This time, the pattern is in pink. Do you notice anything about it? Is it anything like the pattern of the 2 times table?

Quartus is Latin for 'fourth'.
Quadr- comes from the Latin word for 'four'.

4 four   4th fourth

Word	Meaning
quartet	four people singing or playing instruments
quarter	one of four equal parts of a whole
quadruped	a four-legged animal
quadrant	a fourth part or quarter of a circle
quadruplets or quads	four children born at the same birth
square	a flat shape with four equal sides

4 times table

0	x	4	=	0
1	x	4	=	4
2	x	4	=	8
3	x	4	=	12
4	x	4	=	16
5	x	4	=	20
6	x	4	=	24
7	x	4	=	28
8	x	4	=	32
9	x	4	=	36
10	x	4	=	40
11	x	4	=	44
12	x	4	=	48

ALL THE FIVES

1	2	3	4	5	6	7	8	9	10
11	12	13	14	15	16	17	18	19	20
21	22	23	24	25	26	27	28	29	30
31	32	33	34	35	36	37	38	39	40
41	42	43	44	45	46	47	48	49	50
51	52	53	54	55	56	57	58	59	60
61	62	63	64	65	66	67	68	69	70
71	72	73	74	75	76	77	78	79	80
81	82	83	84	85	86	87	88	89	90
91	92	93	94	95	96	97	98	99	100

The 5 times table is in the blue squares. Look at the blue
columns. Do you notice anything about the endings of
the numbers? What is the difference between each
number and the one below it?

Quinque is the Latin
word for 'five'.
Pente is the Greek
word for 'five'.

5 five   5th fifth

Word	Meaning
quintuple	five times as much
quintet	five people singing or playing instruments
quintuplets or quins	five children born at the same birth
pentagon	a five-sided flat shape
pentathlon	an athletic contest with five events for each competitor

5 times table

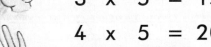

0	x	5	=	0
1	x	5	=	5
2	x	5	=	10
3	x	5	=	15
4	x	5	=	20
5	x	5	=	25
6	x	5	=	30
7	x	5	=	35
8	x	5	=	40
9	x	5	=	45
10	x	5	=	50
11	x	5	=	55
12	x	5	=	60

1	2	3	4	5	6	7	8	9	10
11	12	13	14	15	16	17	18	19	20
21	22	23	24	25	26	27	28	29	30
31	32	33	34	35	36	37	38	39	40
41	42	43	44	45	46	47	48	49	50
51	52	53	54	55	56	57	58	59	60
61	62	63	64	65	66	67	68	69	70
71	72	73	74	75	76	77	78	79	80
81	82	83	84	85	86	87	88	89	90
91	92	93	94	95	96	97	98	99	100

The 6 times table is in the red squares. What is the pattern this time?

6　six　　6th　sixth

Words starting in sex- or hex- come from the Latin and Greek words for 'six'.

Word	Meaning
sextuple	six times as much
sextet	six people singing or playing instruments
sextuplets	six children born at the same birth
sexagenarian	a person of 60 to 69 years old
hexagon	a six-sided flat shape

6 times table

0	x	6	=	0
1	x	6	=	6
2	x	6	=	12
3	x	6	=	18
4	x	6	=	24
5	x	6	=	30
6	x	6	=	36
7	x	6	=	42
8	x	6	=	48
9	x	6	=	54
10	x	6	=	60
11	x	6	=	66
12	x	6	=	72

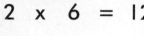
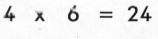

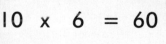

ALL THE SEVENS

1	2	3	4	5	6	7	8	9	10
11	12	13	14	15	16	17	18	19	20
21	22	23	24	25	26	27	28	29	30
31	32	33	34	35	36	37	38	39	40
41	42	43	44	45	46	47	48	49	50
51	52	53	54	55	56	57	58	59	60
61	62	63	64	65	66	67	68	69	70
71	72	73	74	75	76	77	78	79	80
81	82	83	84	85	86	87	88	89	90
91	92	93	94	95	96	97	98	99	100

Look at the green squares this time.

7 seven   7th seventh

Septem is the Latin word for 'seven'.
Hepta is the Greek word for 'seven'.

Word	Meaning
September	in Roman times, the seventh month of the year
septet	seven people singing or playing instruments
septuagenarian	a person of 70 to 79 years old
heptagon	a seven-sided flat shape

7 times table

0	x	7	=	0
1	x	7	=	7
2	x	7	=	14
3	x	7	=	21
4	x	7	=	28
5	x	7	=	35
6	x	7	=	42
7	x	7	=	49
8	x	7	=	56
9	x	7	=	63
10	x	7	=	70
11	x	7	=	77
12	x	7	=	84

ALL THE EIGHTS

1	2	3	4	5	6	7	8	9	10
11	12	13	14	15	16	17	18	19	20
21	22	23	24	25	26	27	28	29	30
31	32	33	34	35	36	37	38	39	40
41	42	43	44	45	46	47	48	49	50
51	52	53	54	55	56	57	58	59	60
61	62	63	64	65	66	67	68	69	70
71	72	73	74	75	76	77	78	79	80
81	82	83	84	85	86	87	88	89	90
91	92	93	94	95	96	97	98	99	100

Look at the numbers in the purple squares. What do you notice about each number and the one below it?

8 eight   8th eighth

Octo is the Greek word for 'eight'.

Word	Meaning
octet	eight people singing or playing instruments
octagon	an eight-sided flat shape
October	in Roman times, the eighth month of the year
octave	a group of eight musical notes
octopus	a sea creature with eight tentacles
octogenarian	a person of 80 to 89 years old

8 times table

0	x	8	=	0
1	x	8	=	8
2	x	8	=	16
3	x	8	=	24
4	x	8	=	32
5	x	8	=	40
6	x	8	=	48
7	x	8	=	56
8	x	8	=	64
9	x	8	=	72
10	x	8	=	80
11	x	8	=	88
12	x	8	=	96

ALL THE NINES

1	2	3	4	5	6	7	8	**9**	10
11	12	13	14	15	16	17	**18**	19	20
21	22	23	24	25	26	**27**	28	29	30
31	32	33	34	35	**36**	37	38	39	40
41	42	43	44	**45**	46	47	48	49	50
51	52	53	**54**	55	56	57	58	59	60
61	62	**63**	64	65	66	67	68	69	70
71	**72**	73	74	75	76	77	78	79	80
81	82	83	84	85	86	87	88	89	**90**
91	92	93	94	95	96	97	98	**99**	100

Look at the numbers in the purple squares. What is the pattern of the tens? What is the pattern of the units?

---

9 nine   9th ninth

Novem is the Latin word for 'nine'. Nonus is the Latin word for 'ninth'.

Word	Meaning
nonet	nine people singing or playing instruments
November	in Roman times, the ninth month of the year
nonagenarian	a person of 90 to 99 years old

9 times table

 0 x 9 = 0

1 x 9 = 9

  2 x 9 = 18

3 x 9 = 27

  4 x 9 = 36

5 x 9 = 45

  6 x 9 = 54

7 x 9 = 63

  8 x 9 = 72

9 x 9 = 81

  10 x 9 = 90

11 x 9 = 99

12 x 9 = 108

ALL THE TENS

1	2	3	4	5	6	7	8	9	10
11	12	13	14	15	16	17	18	19	20
21	22	23	24	25	26	27	28	29	30
31	32	33	34	35	36	37	38	39	40
41	42	43	44	45	46	47	48	49	50
51	52	53	54	55	56	57	58	59	60
61	62	63	64	65	66	67	68	69	70
71	72	73	74	75	76	77	78	79	80
81	82	83	84	85	86	87	88	89	90
91	92	93	94	95	96	97	98	99	100

Find the pattern this time.

10 ten   10th tenth

Decem is the Latin word for 'ten'.

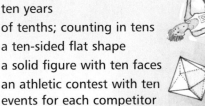

Word	Meaning
decade	ten years
decimal	of tenths; counting in tens
decagon	a ten-sided flat shape
decahedron	a solid figure with ten faces
decathlon	an athletic contest with ten events for each competitor
December	in Roman times, the tenth month of the year

10 times table

0 x 10 = 0
1 x 10 = 10
2 x 10 = 20
3 x 10 = 30
4 x 10 = 40
5 x 10 = 50
6 x 10 = 60
7 x 10 = 70
8 x 10 = 80
9 x 10 = 90
10 x 10 =100
11 x 10 =110
12 x 10 =120

And if you're **really** keen, try learning these tables, too.

11 times table

0	x	11	=	0
1	x	11	=	11
2	x	11	=	22
3	x	11	=	33
4	x	11	=	44
5	x	11	=	55
6	x	11	=	66
7	x	11	=	77
8	x	11	=	88
9	x	11	=	99
10	x	11	=	110
11	x	11	=	121
12	x	11	=	132

12 times table

$0 \times 12 = 0$

$1 \times 12 = 12$

$2 \times 12 = 24$

$3 \times 12 = 36$

$4 \times 12 = 48$

$5 \times 12 = 60$

$6 \times 12 = 72$

$7 \times 12 = 84$

$8 \times 12 = 96$

$9 \times 12 = 108$

$10 \times 12 = 120$

$11 \times 12 = 132$

$12 \times 12 = 144$

EARLY NUMBER SYSTEMS

At first, people used their fingers and thumbs to count, but as trading increased they needed a better system. The first simple records were kept by cutting notches in sticks. Later, people invented different symbols that could be written down.

The ancient Egyptians used simple strokes that they grouped together:

I	II	III	IIII	II II	III	IIII	IIII	III	∩
1	2	3	4	5	6	7	8	9	10

The Babylonians used a similar system, with wedge-shaped symbols.

V	VV	VVV	VVV	VVV	VVV	VVV	VVV	VVV	<
1	2	3	4	5	6	7	8	9	10

The Mayan people lived in Mexico and Central America between about 1500BC until the seventeenth century AD. They used dashes and groups of dots.

•	••	•••	••••	—	•̱	••̱	•••̱	••••̱	=
1	2	3	4	5	6	7	8	9	10

The ancient Greeks used letters of the alphabet.

A	B	Γ	Δ	E	F	Z	I-I	Θ	I
1	2	3	4	5	6	7	8	9	10

The Romans used a combination of letters and strokes.

I	II	III	IV	V	VI	VII	VIII	IX	X
1	2	3	4	5	6	7	8	9	10

The Chinese used a combination of strokes and symbols.

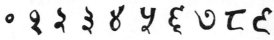

一	二	三	四	五	六	七	八	九	十
1	2	3	4	5	6	7	8	9	10

Early Indian symbols included a zero. The familiar numbers we now use developed from these.

°	९	३	३	४	५	६	७	८	९
1	2	3	4	5	6	7	8	9	10

The familiar numbers we now use are called Arabic numerals because the Arabs introduced them into Europe in the tenth century AD.

0 1 2 3 4 5 6 7 8 9

It took a long time to count and add things up using the old number systems, so people had to find ways to add up more quickly. One of the first 'calculators' was the abacus. This was a frame with rods set in it. Beads were moved along the rods to count and make calculations.

EARLY ALPHABETS

The Greeks and Romans developed their number systems from the alphabet. An alphabet is a writing system that has symbols for speech sounds.

The first people to write things down were the Sumerians, who lived in Mesopotamia (modern-day Iraq) over 5000 years ago. They invented a form of picture writing known as *cuneiform* (wedge-shaped). The ancient Egyptians used a different system of picture writing, known as *hieroglyphics*. The Mayans and Aztecs of Mexico used picture writing called *glyphs*.

Cuneiform

Hieroglyphics

Glyphs

Picture writing used a different symbol for each object. Because so many symbols were needed, picture writing could be hard to understand. The first alphabet with sound symbols rather than pictures was invented about 3600 years ago in the Middle East. Most present-day alphabets were developed from this.

Most languages only have twenty or thirty basic sounds, so it is quick and easy to learn an alphabet.

How the alphabet developed

First alphabet (North Semitic)

Phoenician

Early Greek

Classical Greek

Roman

The name 'alphabet' comes from the Greek words alpha and beta. These are the first two letters of the Greek alphabet.

MEASURING THROUGH THE AGES

When people began building and trading, they had to find ways of measuring things. The ancient Egyptians used their hands and bodies for measuring.

1 digit = 1.9 cm
4 digits = 1 palm = 7.6 cm
3 palms = 1 span = 22.8 cm
2 spans = 1 cubit = 45.6 cm
4 cubits = 1 stature = 182.4 cm

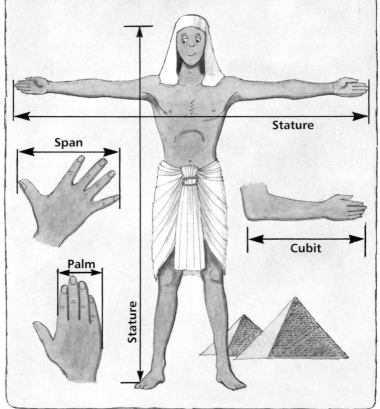

Stature

Span

Cubit

Palm

Stature

The ancient Romans introduced some measurements for length and distance.

1 pace = 1.5 m (the distance covered by two complete steps)

1 stadium = 184.7 m (the length of an athletics stadium)

1 Roman mile = 1000 paces = 1.5 km (The word 'mile' comes from the Latin word *mille*, meaning 'thousand'.)

In England, new measurements were introduced during the reign of King Henry I (1100–1135). The distance from the king's nose to his fingertip was called a yard.

3 feet = 1 yard
12 inches = 1 foot
4 inches = 1 hand

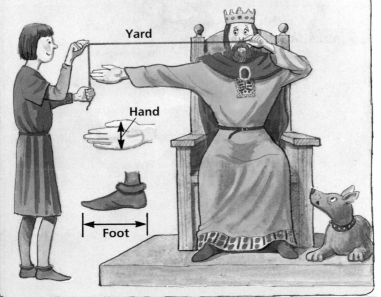

IMPERIAL MEASUREMENTS

The measurements introduced in the twelfth century formed the basis for the imperial system of measuring, established in Britain in 1824. When a standard yard was fixed, other measurements of length were based on it.

22 yards = 1 chain   10 chains = 1 furlong
1760 yards (8 furlongs) = 1 mile (the imperial mile was adapted from the Roman mile)
1 fathom (used for measuring the depth of water) = 6 feet, or 2 yards

Weight

The imperial system set standards for measuring other things besides length. The smallest unit of weight was 1 grain (based on the weight of a single grain of corn, about 0.064 grams).

24 grains = 1 pennyweight (the weight of a penny coin)
27.34 grains = 1 dram (based on the drachma, an ancient Greek silver coin)
16 drams = 1 ounce
16 ounces = 1 pound
14 pounds = 1 stone

Capacity

The basic units for dry measure were the peck and the
bushel. (A peck was a container for holding dry goods,
and a bushel was a larger container.) The basic units for
liquid measure were the pint and the gallon.

> 4 gills = 1 pint
> 8 pints = 1 gallon
> 2 gallons = 1 peck
> 4 pecks = 1 bushel

MEASURING TODAY

The metric system was devised in France in the 18th century and was officially adopted there in 1799. The change to metrication in the United Kingdom began in the 1970s. The metric system is now used more often than imperial measurements, though you will still see imperial measurements in shops.

The standard *metre* (the name comes from *metrum*, the Latin word for 'measure') was based on $\frac{1}{10\,000\,000}$ of the distance from the North Pole to the Equator on a line passing through Paris.

The *litre* (liquid measure) was the capacity of a cube with sides $\frac{1}{10}$ of a metre.

A *gram* (dry measure) was $\frac{1}{1000}$ of the weight of a litre of water at 4° centigrade.

In 1963 the Weights and Measures Act defined the following equivalents between imperial and metric measurements.

Distance

1 inch = 25.4 millimetres or 2.54 centimetres
1 yard = 0.91 metres
1 mile = 1.609 kilometres

Weight

mg   1000 milligrams = 1 gram

g   1000 grams   = 1 kilogram

kg   1000 kilograms = 1 tonne

Use grams to buy butter or cheese.

Use kilograms to buy potatoes.

Use tonnes to buy gravel for
a path, or sand for a sandpit.

Metric/Imperial equivalents

1 g = 0.035 ounces (oz)	1 oz = 28.35 g
1 kg = 2.205 pounds (lb)	1 lb = 0.4536 kg
	1 stone = 6.35 kg
1 tonne = 0.984 tons	1 ton = 1.016 tonnes

How much do you weigh? The heaviest man in history,
Jon Minnoch of Washington State, USA (1941–1983)
weighed 635 kg (100 stones). An African bull elephant,
the heaviest land mammal, can weigh as much as 7000 kg
(about 7 tons).

Length

mm	10 millimetres	= 1 centimetre
cm	100 centimetres	= 1 metre
m	1000 metres	= 1 kilometre km

How tall are you? Do you know your height in centimetres or in feet and inches?

Metric/Imperial equivalents

1 mm = 0.04 inch (in)   1 in = 25.4 mm or 2.54 cm
1 cm = 0.4 in   1 ft = 30.5 cm or 0.305 m
1 m = 3.28 feet (ft)
     or 1.09 yards (yds)   1 yd = 91.4 cm or 0.914 m
1 km = 0.62 miles   1 mile = 1.61 km

The tallest man in history was Robert Wadlow (1918–1940), from Illinois, USA. He grew to be 272 cm (8 ft 11 in) tall. By the age of five he was 164 cm (5 ft 4 in), and he was 196 cm (6 ft 5 in) by the time he was ten.

The tallest living woman is 231.7 cm (7 ft 7¼ in). She was 190.5 cm (6 ft 3 in) by the time she was ten years old.

The longest rivers in the world are the Amazon in South America (6280 km/3900 miles) and the Nile in Egypt, North Africa (6670 km/4135 miles).

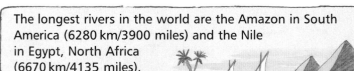

Capacity

ml	10 millilitres	= 1 centilitre
cl	10 centilitres	= 1 decilitre
dl	10 decilitres	= 1 litre
l	10 litres	= 1 decalitre
dal	10 decalitres	= 1 hectolitre hl

People still buy milk in pints. Which other imperial measures of capacity have you seen?

Metric/Imperial equivalents

1 ml = 0.002 pint (pt) or 0.04 fluid ounces (fl oz)

1 fl oz = 28.4 ml   1 decilitre = 0.0176 pt or 0.35 fl oz

1 pt = 568 ml or 0.568 litre

1 litre = 1.76 pts   1 gallon = 4.54 litres

1 decalitre = 2.20 gallons

The largest known dinosaur eggs are those of *Hypselosaurus priscus* ('high ridge lizard'), which lived 80 million years ago. Examples found in France in 1961 have a capacity of 3.3 litres (5.8 pts).

Area

Here are ways to calculate the areas of different shapes.

A square
Multiply one side by another:
6 x 6 = 36 sq cm

A rectangle
Multiply the width by the
length: 6 x 10 = 60 sq cm

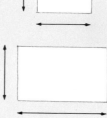

A triangle
Multiply the base by the height
and divide the answer by 2.

10 x 15 = $\frac{150}{2}$ = 75 sq cm

The Great Barrier Reef, off Queensland in northeastern
Australia, is the largest structure ever built by
living creatures. It consists of billions of
living and dead stony corals, and it has
taken about 600 million years to
reach its present size. It is over 2000km
(1240 miles) long and covers an area
of 207,000 sq km (80,109 sq miles).

FRACTIONS AND DECIMALS

If you divide an orange into separate parts, each part is a fraction of the whole orange. Fractions can also be expressed as decimals.

Fractions	**Decimals**
Parts of a whole	*Number shown in tenths*
$\frac{1}{10}$	0.1
$\frac{1}{100}$	0.01
$\frac{1}{1000}$	0.001
$\frac{1}{4}$	0.25
$\frac{1}{2}$	0.50
$\frac{3}{4}$	0.75
$\frac{1}{8}$	0.125
$\frac{1}{16}$	0.062
$\frac{1}{32}$	0.031
$\frac{1}{3}$	0.333
$\frac{2}{3}$	0.666

TEMPERATURE

There are two scales for measuring temperature. One is Fahrenheit, named after a German physicist, Gabriel Fahrenheit (1686–1736). Until recently, this was the scale normally used to measure temperature in the UK. Now, however, Centigrade or Celsius, named after the Swedish astronomer Anders Celsius (1701–1744), is more common.

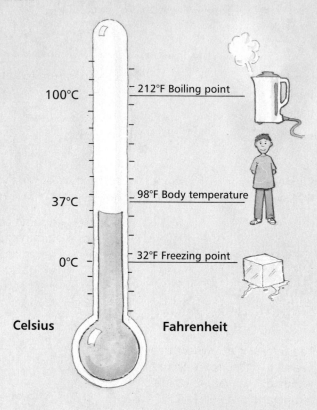

100°C — 212°F Boiling point

37°C — 98°F Body temperature

0°C — 32°F Freezing point

Celsius **Fahrenheit**

Why do we *need* to know the temperature of things?

The normal body temperature of a human being is about 98.4°F/36.9°C. Illness can make it go up

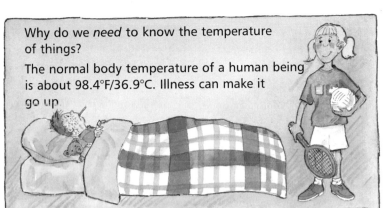

Food has to be cooked at the right temperature to get the best results and be safe to eat.

We need to know the temperature of the air outside so that we can be prepared for very hot or very cold weather.

On an average summer day in Britain, the temperature is usually in the region of 70°F/20°C. The highest temperature ever recorded was 136°F/58°C in Libya in 1922.

The coldest place where people live all the time is the Siberian village of Oymyakon, where a temperature of −98°F/−72°C has been recorded.

DIVIDING THE DAY

The first 'clock' was the sun. People noticed that the sun changed its position in the sky as the day went on. Then some people must have noticed that a tall, straight object, such as a stick in the ground, casts a long shadow that moves in a regular pattern throughout the day.

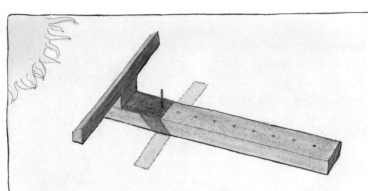

The ancient Egyptians invented the first shadow clock.
They divided the day into twelve equal parts, which
they marked on the clock. The hour came from this
early clock. The clock was pointed at the sun. The
crossbar's shadow was thrown onto the hour scale.

Simple sundials were first used in Egypt about 3500 BC.
They were the main way of telling the time for centuries.

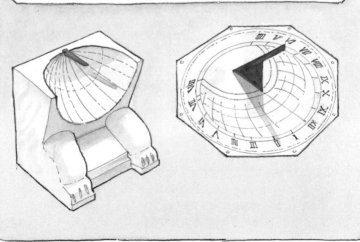

DIVIDING THE YEAR

Ancient people knew that the weather changed during the year and that there was a cycle of seasons. The whole cycle forms a year, the time it takes for the Earth to travel round the sun.

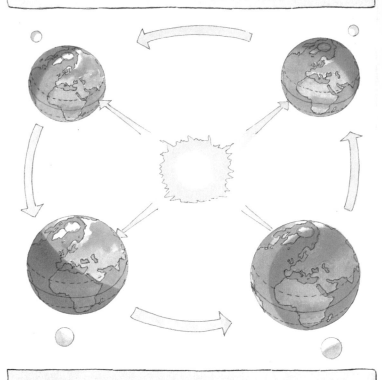

People tried to calculate the exact length of a year. This was difficult because the Earth takes 365.25 days to orbit the sun but the moon only takes 354 days to orbit the Earth twelve times. So exactly how long *is* a year?

They also noticed the moon and saw that it seemed to grow from a thin crescent to a full moon, in a regular pattern. This happened about twelve times during a cycle of seasons. The time the moon takes to change from crescent to full, during which it completes one orbit round the Earth while spinning on its axis, is called a month.

The Babylonians divided the month into four seven-day periods, or weeks.

CALENDARS

Different peoples found different ways of measuring the year and making calendars.

The ancient Chinese had a 360-day year divided into twelve months. This was a bit shorter than the sun's year, so they sometimes had to add an extra month.

The Babylonians also had a 360-day year. They added three months every eight years to keep their calendar accurate. The ancient Egyptians were the most accurate, with a 365-day year. They had to add an extra day every four years. This is the system we use today.

People needed calendars to measure the year and also to set dates for festivals and other events. The Mayan people of Mexico and Central America had a very accurate calendar of 365 days, plus a separate calendar of holy days.

There are still different calendars in different parts of the world. The Gregorian calendar is the one used in most of the western world. It was named after Pope Gregory, who introduced it in 1582. It is a solar (sun) calendar with 365 days in the year, divided into twelve months. An extra day is added every four years, to make a leap year. The Jewish calendar has twelve 29-day and 30-day months.

Hindus follow a lunar (moon) calendar of twelve months and add extra months to keep in line with the solar year. Muslims have a 354-day year.

Leap Years

To find out which is a leap year, divide the number of the year by four. The numbers of leap years divide exactly, eg 1996, 2000, 2004, 2008.

Days in the Month

Thirty days hath September,
April, June and November.
All the rest have thirty one
Except in February alone,
Which has twenty eight days clear,
And twenty nine in each leap year.

MEASURING TIME

There were several different types of early clocks. One of the first, used by the ancient Greeks, was a simple water clock called a *clepsydra*. Water ran at a steady rate from one bowl into another bowl, which had different levels marked on it.

Candle clocks were also used in early times. A candle was marked with hours and people read the time as the candle burnt down.

Mechanical clocks, with weight-driven mechanisms, were invented in Europe in the tenth century. Spring-operated clocks came later, in the fifteenth century. They were much smaller than the earlier clocks.

Early clocks only had an hour hand. Clocks with a minute hand first appeared in 1670. The first wristwatches were made in the United States in the late 19th century.

60 seconds	=	1 minute	12 months	=	1 year
60 minutes	=	1 hour	365 days	=	1 year
24 hours	=	1 day	366 days	=	1 leap year
7 days	=	1 week	10 years	=	1 decade
4 weeks	=	1 month	100 years	=	1 century

From midnight to before noon
= morning
= *ante meridiem*
= a m

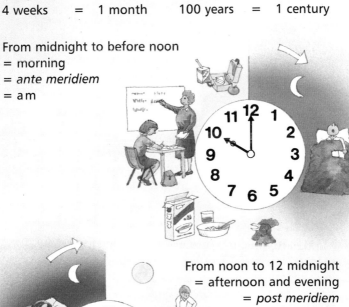

From noon to 12 midnight
= afternoon and evening
= *post meridiem*
= p m

Meridies
is the Latin word
for 'noon'.
Ante means 'before'.
Post means 'after'.

24-HOUR CLOCK

Bus, rail, sea and air timetables use a 24-hour clock. Many digital clocks and watches also display the time in this way.

00.00 or 24.00	=	12 o'clock midnight	12.00 =	12 o'clock midday
01.00	=	1 am	13.00 =	1 pm
02.00	=	2 am	14.00 =	2 pm
03.00	=	3 am	15.00 =	3 pm
04.00	=	4 am	16.00 =	4 pm
05.00	=	5 am	17.00 =	5 pm
06.00	=	6 am	18.00 =	6 pm
07.00	=	7 am	19.00 =	7 pm
08.00	=	8 am	20.00 =	8 pm
09.00	=	9 am	21.00 =	9 pm
10.00	=	10 am	22.00 =	10 pm
11.00	=	11 am	23.00 =	11 pm

WORLD TIME ZONES

Because the Earth takes 24 hours to do a full rotation on its axis, when the sun is rising in one part of the world it is still nighttime in other places. In order to know the time in other parts of the world, several countries agreed to establish world time zones in the late nineteenth century. All world times are based on Greenwich Mean Time – the time in Greenwich, near London, which is at 0° longitude on the globe. Each additional 15° longitude from Greenwich represents one hour later to the east and one hour earlier to the west. When clocks in the UK are put forward one hour for British Summer Time, the time in the UK is the same as that in the next time zone to the east. There are 24 time zones altogether.

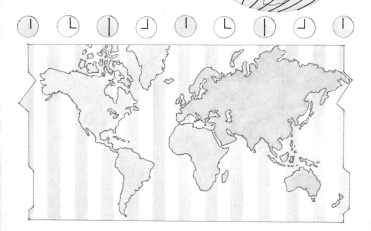

OVEN TEMPERATURES

Gas Mark	Temperature		Heat of oven
	C	F	
$\frac{1}{4}$	110°	225°	very cool
$\frac{1}{2}$	120°	250°	very cool
1	140°	275°	cool
2	150°	300°	cool
3	160°	325°	warm
4	180°	350°	moderate
5	190°	375°	moderately hot
6	200°	400°	hot
7	220°	425°	hot
8	230°	450°	very hot
9	240°	475°	very hot

WASHING INSTRUCTIONS

Washtub symbols now in use are shown on the left of the table below. The number given in each symbol is the most effective wash temperature in degrees C.

A washtub without a bar shows that maximum washing conditions may be used at the temperature given.

A washtub with just one bar beneath it shows that medium washing conditions should be used with reduced agitation and spinning. This is sometimes labelled 'wash as synthetic'.

A washtub with two bars underneath shows that minimum washing conditions should be used. This is sometimes labelled 'wash as wool'.

Symbol	Temp: Machine	Temp: Hand	Agitation	Rinse	Spinning Wringing
95	very hot 95° to boil	hand-hot 50°C or boil	maximum	normal	normal
60	hot 60°C	hand-hot 50°C	maximum	normal	normal
50	hand-hot 50°C	hand-hot 50°C	medium	cold	short spin or drip dry
40	warm 40°C	warm 40°C	maximum	normal	normal
40	warm 40°C	warm 40°C	minimum	cold	short spin
40	warm 40°C	warm 40°C	minimum do not rub	normal	normal spin, do not hand wring
30 / 30	cool 30°C	cool 30°C	minimum	cold	short spin, do not hand wring

COMPARATIVE CLOTHING SIZES

Shirts

UK/USA

inches	12	12½	13	13½	14	14½	15	15½	16	16½	17	17½

UK/Europe

centimetres	30-31	32	33	34-35	36	37	38	39-40	41	42	43	44-45

Ladies Clothes

UK

size code	10	12	14	16	18	20	22
bust/hip inches	32/35	34/37	36/39	38/41	40/43	42/45	44/47
bust/hip centimetres	84/89	88/94	92/99	97/104	102/109	107/114	112/119

USA

size code	10	12	14	16	18	20	22
bust/hip inches	35/37½	36/38	37½/40	39/41½	40½/43	42½/45	44½/47

(European sizes vary from country to country)

Children's Clothes

UK

Age	1	2	3	4	5	6	7	8	9	10	11	12
height – inches	32	36	38	40	43	45	48	50	53	55	58	60
centimetres	80	92	98	104	110	116	122	128	134	140	146	152

USA

boys' size code	1	2	3	4	5	6	8		10	12
girls' size code	2	3	4	5	6	6x	7	8	10	12

Europe

height – centimetres	80	92	98	104	110	116	122	128	134	140	146	152

COMPARATIVE SHOE SIZES

(All sizes are approximate)

Men's Shoe Sizes

British	7	7½	8	8½	9	9½	10	10½	11
American	8	8½	9	9½	10	10½	11	11½	11½
Continental	40	41	42	43	43	44	44	45	45

Women's Shoe Sizes

British	4	4½	5	5½	6	6½	7
American	5½	6	6½	7	7½	8	8½
Continental	36	37	38	39	39½	40	41

Children's Shoe Sizes

British	2	3	4	4½	5	6	7	8	8½
American	3½	4½	5	6	7	7½	8½	9	10
Continental	18	19	20	21	22	23	24	25	26

Children's Shoe Sizes (cont'd)

British	9	10	11	12	12½	13
American	11	11½	12½	13	1	1½
Continental	27	28	29	30	31	32

WORLD CURRENCIES

COUNTRY	CURRENCY
ALGERIA	dinar
AUSTRALIA	dollars
AUSTRIA	schillings
CANADA	dollars
DENMARK	kroner
EGYPT	Egyptian pounds
EIRE	Irish pounds (punts)
FRANCE	francs
GERMANY	Deutschmarks
GHANA	cedi
GREAT BRITAIN	pounds sterling
GREECE	drachma
HONG KONG	dollars
INDIA	rupees
ITALY	lire
JAPAN	yen
KENYA	shillings
KUWAIT	dinar
LEBANON	pounds
MALAYSIA	ringgits (Malaysian dollars)
MALTA	Maltese pounds
MEXICO	pesos
MOROCCO	dirham
NETHERLANDS	guilders
NEW ZEALAND	dollars
NIGERIA	naira
PAKISTAN	rupees
PHILIPPINES	pesos
PORTUGAL	escudos
SAUDI ARABIA	riyals
SINGAPORE	dollars
SOUTH AFRICA	rand
SPAIN	pesetas
TUNISIA	dinar
TURKEY	liras
USA	dollars
ZAIRE	zaire

INTERESTING NUMBER FACTS

- If a person could jump as well as a flea, he or she would be able to jump over St Paul's Cathedral – 110 m.

- There are 1,832,000 doctors in China, more than in any other country in the world.

- A blind person using Braille needs one hour to read 3000 words.

- A daily newspaper may contain 100,000 words (not including advertisements) – the equivalent of a 200-page novel.

- Swarms of locusts can number 40,000,000,000 insects and can weigh 72,000 tonnes. They move at 16 – 19 kph (10 – 12 mph).

- The largest creature ever to inhabit the Earth is the blue whale, which weighs 2.7 tonnes at birth and measures 8 m (26 ft) in length. A full grown blue whale can be 30 m (98 ft) long and weigh 136 tonnes – as heavy as 2000 people!

- The first American moon landing, in July 1969, cost approximately $20,000,000,000.

- The coldest place in the world is Antarctica, where the temperature can go as low as –57°C (–70°F). The hottest place in the world is the Sahara Desert in North Africa, where temperatures as high as 57°C (136°F) have been recorded.

- The slowest-growing animal is the deep-sea clam, which takes 100 years to reach a length of 8 mm (⅓ in).

- The tallest statue in the world is of the Sioux Indian Chief Crazy Horse, on Thunderhead Mountain in South Dakota, USA. It is 172 m (564 ft) high and 195 m (640 ft) long.

- The King James Bible has 50 authors, 66 books, 1189 chapters and 31,173 verses.

- A sneeze can travel up to 160 kph (100 mph).

- A human being has more than 600 muscles – but a caterpillar can have as many as 2000 muscles!

- The sun is 330,330 times larger than the Earth.

- An ordinary pencil can draw a line 55 km (35 miles) long, or write about 50,000 English words.

- The average person in Britain eats 7.4 kg (16 lbs) of chocolate every year.

- The area of Russia, the largest country in the world, is 17,075,400 sq km (6,593,391 sq miles). The Vatican City, in Rome, the smallest country in the world, has an area of only 0.44 sq km (0.17 sq miles).